BASIC MATH DRILLS

1st Grade

{SUBTRACTION}

SPI MATH
WORKBOOKS

ISBN-13:
978-1540716149

ISBN-10:
1540716147

9 – 8 = ____

8 – 4 = ____

6 – 4 = ____

10 – 4 = ____

8 – 5 = ____

13 – 9 = ____

3 – 3 = ____

6 – 1 = ____

5 – 4 = ____

7 – 5 = ____

18 – 8 = ____

13 – 5 = ____

12 – 7 = ____

9 – 1 = ____

14 – 4 = ____

4 – 4 = ____

16 – 6 = ____

17 – 7 = ____

10 – 0 = ____

15 – 5 = ____

Answer Key

$9 - 8 = \underline{\ 1\ }$

$8 - 4 = \underline{\ 4\ }$

$6 - 4 = \underline{\ 2\ }$

$10 - 4 = \underline{\ 6\ }$

$8 - 5 = \underline{\ 3\ }$

$13 - 9 = \underline{\ 4\ }$

$3 - 3 = \underline{\ 0\ }$

$6 - 1 = \underline{\ 5\ }$

$5 - 4 = \underline{\ 1\ }$

$7 - 5 = \underline{\ 2\ }$

$18 - 8 = \underline{\ 10\ }$

$13 - 5 = \underline{\ 8\ }$

$12 - 7 = \underline{\ 5\ }$

$9 - 1 = \underline{\ 8\ }$

$14 - 4 = \underline{\ 10\ }$

$4 - 4 = \underline{\ 0\ }$

$16 - 6 = \underline{\ 10\ }$

$17 - 7 = \underline{\ 10\ }$

$10 - 0 = \underline{\ 10\ }$

$15 - 5 = \underline{\ 10\ }$

99		97	96	95	94	93	92		90
89	88	87		85	84	83	82	81	80
79	78	77	76	75	74		72	71	70
69	68		66	65	64	63	62		
59	58	57	56	55	54	53	52	51	50
49	48		46	45	44		42	41	40
39	38	37	36		34	33	32	31	30
29			26	25		23	22	21	20
19	18	17	16	15	14	13		11	10
9	8	7			4	3	2	1	0

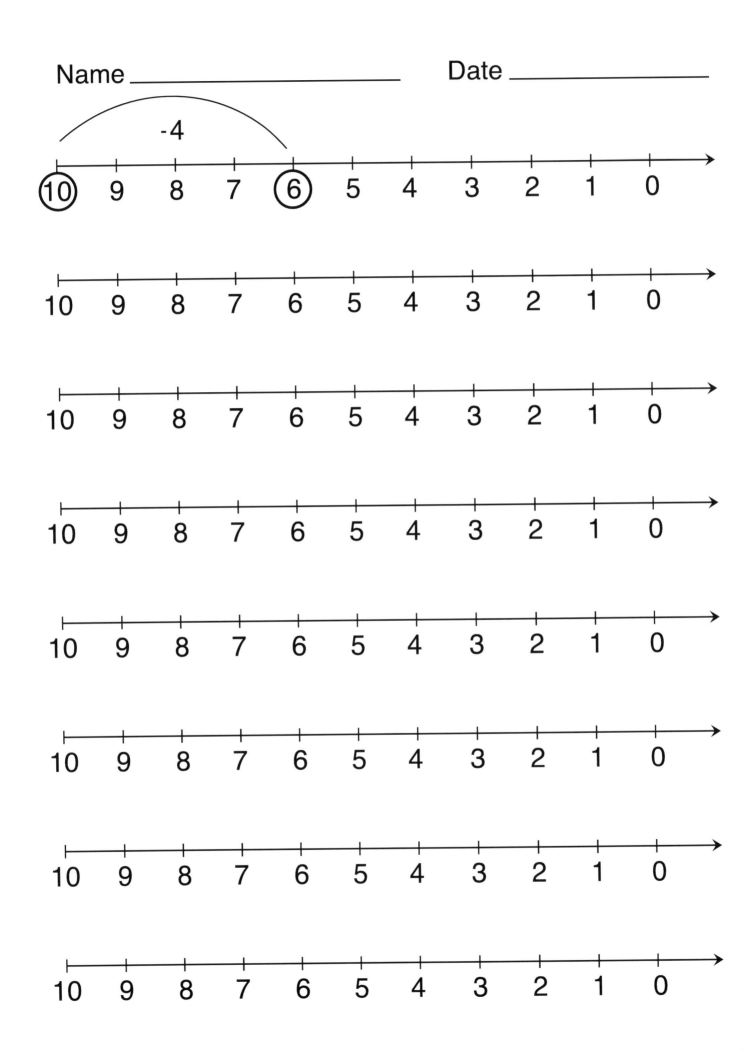

11 – 5 = _____

7 – 5 = _____

4 – 3 = _____

3 – 2 = _____

10 – 4 = _____

10 – 9 = _____

4 – 1 = _____

10 – 3 = _____

9 – 1 = _____

5 – 2 = _____

5 – 3 = _____

6 – 1 = _____

9 – 3 = _____

8 – 2 = _____

12 – 3 = _____

15 – 8 = _____

14 – 6 = _____

4 – 4 = _____

10 – 7 = _____

10 – 2 = _____

Answer Key

$11 - 5 = \underline{\quad 6 \quad}$

$7 - 5 = \underline{\quad 2 \quad}$

$4 - 3 = \underline{\quad 1 \quad}$

$3 - 2 = \underline{\quad 1 \quad}$

$10 - 4 = \underline{\quad 6 \quad}$

$10 - 9 = \underline{\quad 1 \quad}$

$4 - 1 = \underline{\quad 3 \quad}$

$10 - 3 = \underline{\quad 7 \quad}$

$9 - 1 = \underline{\quad 8 \quad}$

$5 - 2 = \underline{\quad 3 \quad}$

$5 - 3 = \underline{\quad 2 \quad}$

$6 - 1 = \underline{\quad 5 \quad}$

$9 - 3 = \underline{\quad 6 \quad}$

$8 - 2 = \underline{\quad 6 \quad}$

$12 - 3 = \underline{\quad 9 \quad}$

$15 - 8 = \underline{\quad 7 \quad}$

$14 - 6 = \underline{\quad 8 \quad}$

$4 - 4 = \underline{\quad 0 \quad}$

$10 - 7 = \underline{\quad 3 \quad}$

$10 - 2 = \underline{\quad 8 \quad}$

Name _____   Date _____

99				95	94	93	92	91	90
89	88	87	86			83	82	81	80
79			76		74	73		71	70
69	68		66		64	63		61	60
59	58			55	54		52	51	50
49			46	45	44	43	42	41	40
39	38		36	35	34	33			
29	28	27	26	25		23	22	21	20
		17	16		14	13	12	11	10
9	8	7	6	5	4		2	1	

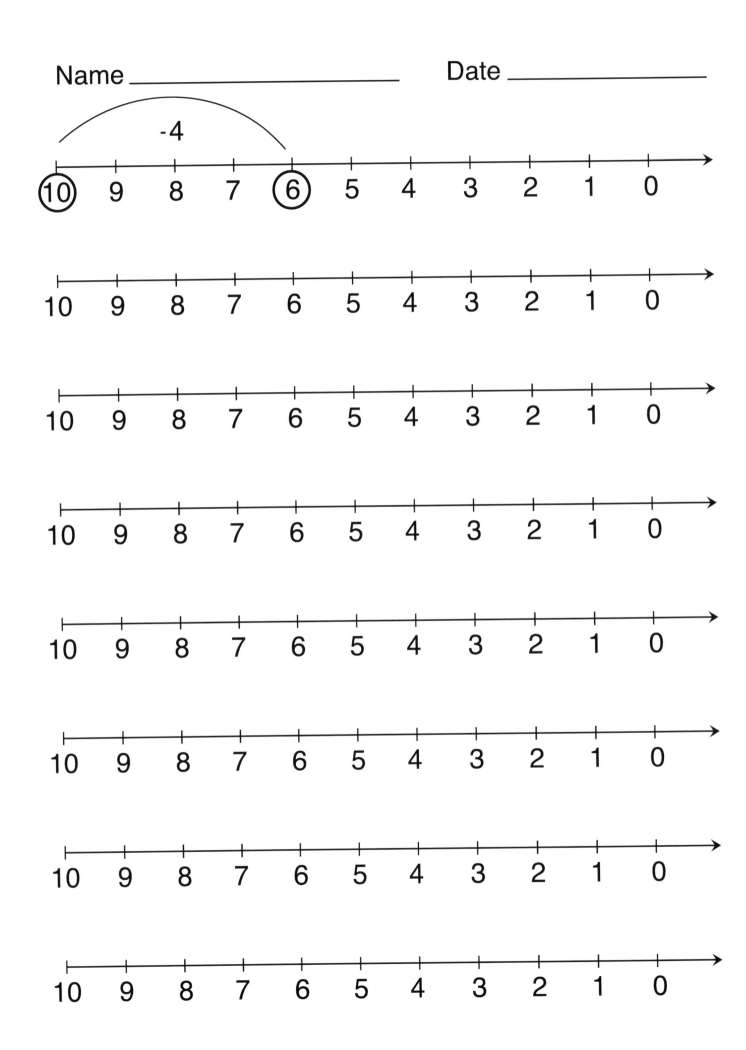

10 − 4 = _____   10 − 2 = _____

12 − 6 = _____   8 − 7 = _____

4 − 2 = _____   7 − 5 = _____

6 − 4 = _____   5 − 4 = _____

6 − 6 = _____   3 − 1 = _____

18 − 9 = _____   2 − 1 = _____

11 − 8 = _____   9 − 1 = _____

1 − 1 = _____   11 − 7 = _____

5 − 0 = _____   8 − 5 = _____

11 − 6 = _____   9 − 3 = _____

Answer Key

$10 - 4 = \underline{6}$

$12 - 6 = \underline{6}$

$4 - 2 = \underline{2}$

$6 - 4 = \underline{2}$

$6 - 6 = \underline{0}$

$18 - 9 = \underline{9}$

$11 - 8 = \underline{3}$

$1 - 1 = \underline{0}$

$5 - 0 = \underline{5}$

$11 - 6 = \underline{5}$

$10 - 2 = \underline{8}$

$8 - 7 = \underline{1}$

$7 - 5 = \underline{2}$

$5 - 4 = \underline{1}$

$3 - 1 = \underline{2}$

$2 - 1 = \underline{1}$

$9 - 1 = \underline{8}$

$11 - 7 = \underline{4}$

$8 - 5 = \underline{3}$

$9 - 3 = \underline{6}$

99						93	92		90
89				85	84	83		81	80
	78	77		75	74	73	72	71	70
69					64		62	61	60
59		57	56				52	51	
	48	47				43	42	41	40
39	38	37	36	35	34				
		27	26	25	24	23	22	21	20
19	18	17					12	11	
	8	7			4			1	0

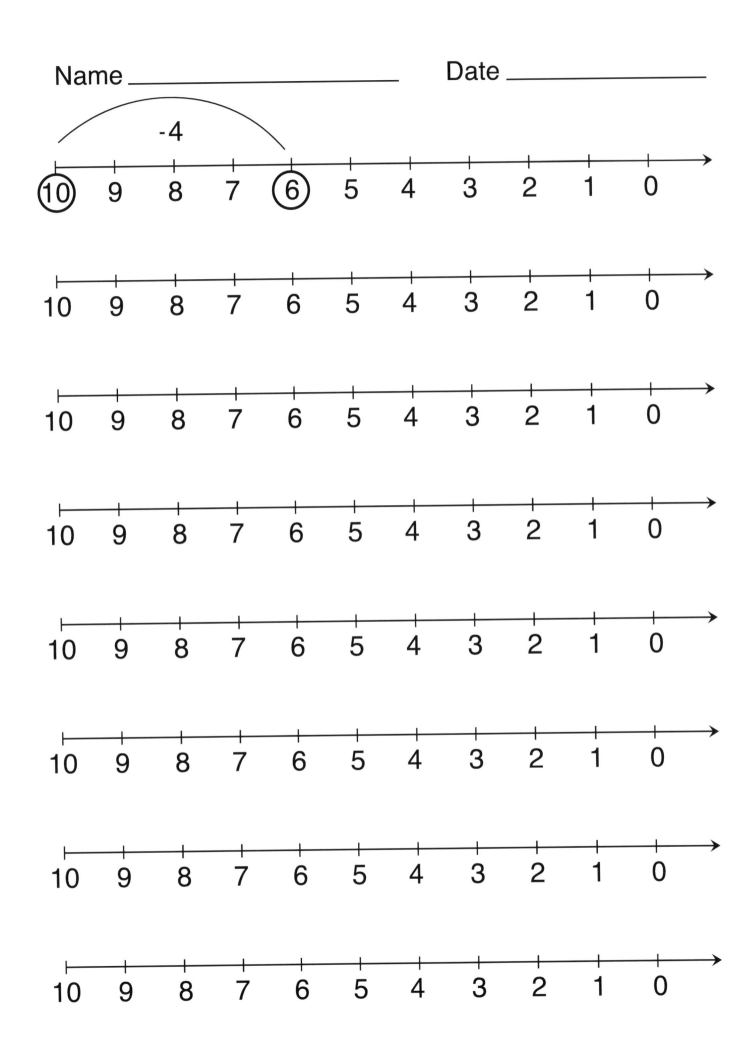

4 – 0 = _____

5 – 3 = _____

9 – 2 = _____

6 – 5 = _____

18 – 9 = _____

13 – 5 = _____

6 – 3 = _____

10 – 7 = _____

10 – 9 = _____

3 – 0 = _____

6 – 0 = _____

11 – 7 = _____

14 – 8 = _____

7 – 6 = _____

8 – 2 = _____

13 – 4 = _____

4 – 1 = _____

9 – 5 = _____

17 – 9 = _____

11 – 2 = _____

Answer Key

$4 - 0 = \underline{4}$ $6 - 0 = \underline{6}$

$5 - 3 = \underline{2}$ $11 - 7 = \underline{4}$

$9 - 2 = \underline{7}$ $14 - 8 = \underline{6}$

$6 - 5 = \underline{1}$ $7 - 6 = \underline{1}$

$18 - 9 = \underline{9}$ $8 - 2 = \underline{6}$

$13 - 5 = \underline{8}$ $13 - 4 = \underline{9}$

$6 - 3 = \underline{3}$ $4 - 1 = \underline{3}$

$10 - 7 = \underline{3}$ $9 - 5 = \underline{4}$

$10 - 9 = \underline{1}$ $17 - 9 = \underline{8}$

$3 - 0 = \underline{3}$ $11 - 2 = \underline{9}$

99							92	91	90
89		87			84		82		
79				74			72	71	70
		67		65					60
59		57					52		
49		47		45					40
39				35			32		30
						23		21	
			16		14		12		10
	8		6	5	4	3			

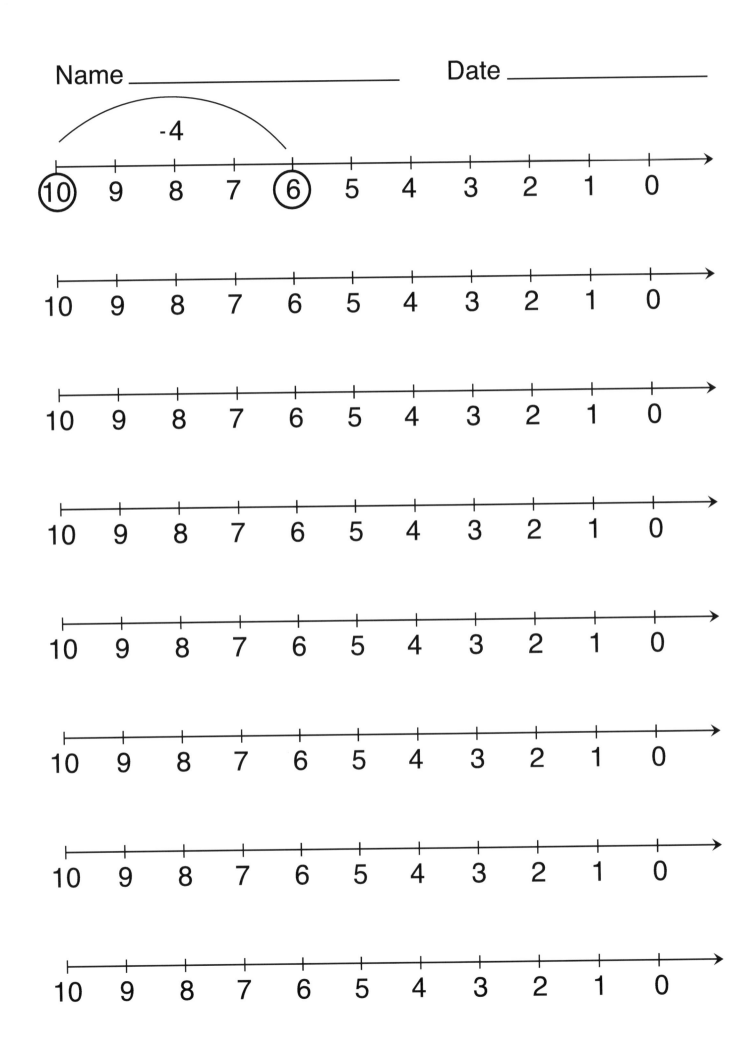

4 − 1 = ___

12 − 4 = ___

6 − 0 = ___

12 − 8 = ___

13 − 6 = ___

5 − 2 = ___

9 − 7 = ___

5 − 5 = ___

6 − 2 = ___

6 − 3 = ___

12 − 6 = ___

14 − 5 = ___

8 − 5 = ___

12 − 7 = ___

13 − 7 = ___

0 − 0 = ___

3 − 2 = ___

6 − 1 = ___

14 − 9 = ___

8 − 2 = ___

Answer Key

4 – 1 = __3__

12 – 4 = __8__

6 – 0 = __6__

12 – 8 = __4__

13 – 6 = __7__

5 – 2 = __3__

9 – 7 = __2__

5 – 5 = __0__

6 – 2 = __4__

6 – 3 = __3__

12 – 6 = __6__

14 – 5 = __9__

8 – 5 = __3__

12 – 7 = __5__

13 – 7 = __6__

0 – 0 = __0__

3 – 2 = __1__

6 – 1 = __5__

14 – 9 = __5__

8 – 2 = __6__

			96						90
89	88			85					
79					74	73		71	
69					64	63	62	61	
59	58	57	56	55		53	52	51	
49					44	43	42	41	40
39	38	37	36		34				
29		27	26		24	23	22	21	20
19		17						11	10
9		7	6		4	3		1	0

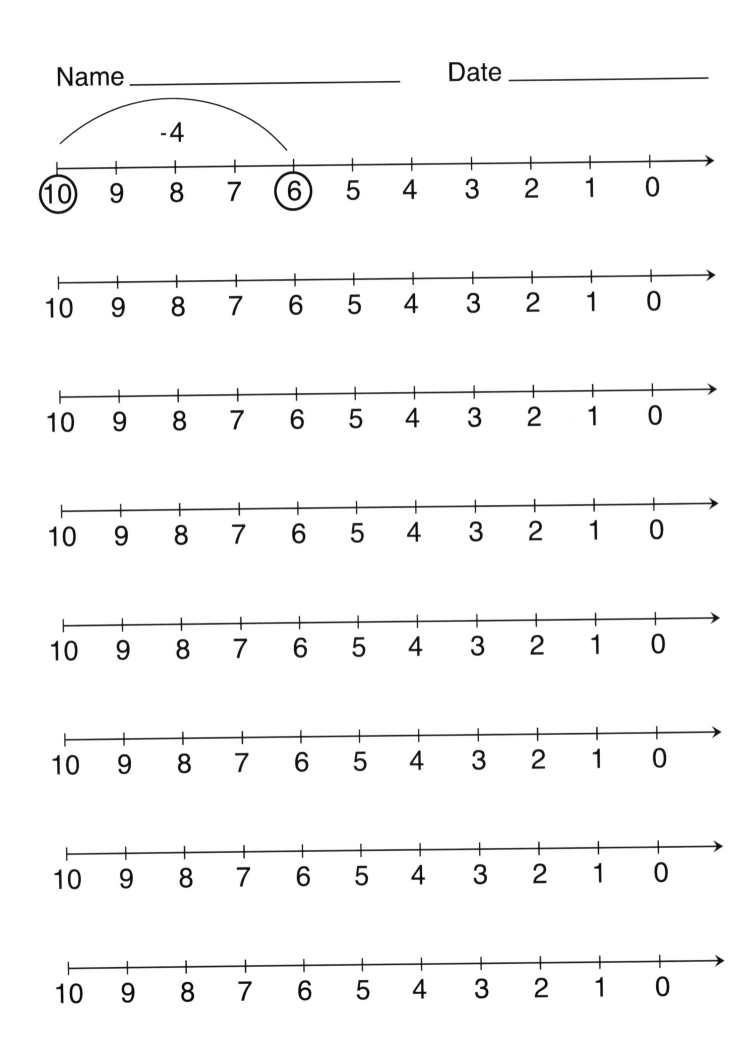

-4

10 9 8 7 6 5 4 3 2 1 0

10 9 8 7 6 5 4 3 2 1 0

10 9 8 7 6 5 4 3 2 1 0

10 9 8 7 6 5 4 3 2 1 0

10 9 8 7 6 5 4 3 2 1 0

10 9 8 7 6 5 4 3 2 1 0

10 9 8 7 6 5 4 3 2 1 0

9 – 1 = ____

8 – 4 = ____

7 – 5 = ____

11 – 6 = ____

12 – 7 = ____

5 – 3 = ____

12 – 8 = ____

13 – 9 = ____

3 – 1 = ____

18 – 9 = ____

15 – 6 = ____

10 – 6 = ____

7 – 2 = ____

7 – 6 = ____

13 – 5 = ____

8 – 8 = ____

7 – 4 = ____

16 – 7 = ____

12 – 3 = ____

5 – 1 = ____

Answer Key

$9 - 1 = \underline{8}$

$15 - 6 = \underline{9}$

$8 - 4 = \underline{4}$

$10 - 6 = \underline{4}$

$7 - 5 = \underline{2}$

$7 - 2 = \underline{5}$

$11 - 6 = \underline{5}$

$7 - 6 = \underline{1}$

$12 - 7 = \underline{5}$

$13 - 5 = \underline{8}$

$5 - 3 = \underline{2}$

$8 - 8 = \underline{0}$

$12 - 8 = \underline{4}$

$7 - 4 = \underline{3}$

$13 - 9 = \underline{4}$

$16 - 7 = \underline{9}$

$3 - 1 = \underline{2}$

$12 - 3 = \underline{9}$

$18 - 9 = \underline{9}$

$5 - 1 = \underline{4}$

Name _____ Date _____

199	198		196	195	194	193	192	191	190
189	188	187		185	184	183	182	181	180
179		177	176	175	174	173	172	171	170
169	168	167	166	165		163	162		160
159	158	157	156	155	154		152	151	150
149		147	146		144	143	142	141	140
139	138		136	135	134	133	132	131	130
129	128	127	126	125	124	123	122	121	120
119		117	116		114	113	112	111	110
109	108	107	106	105	104	103	102		100

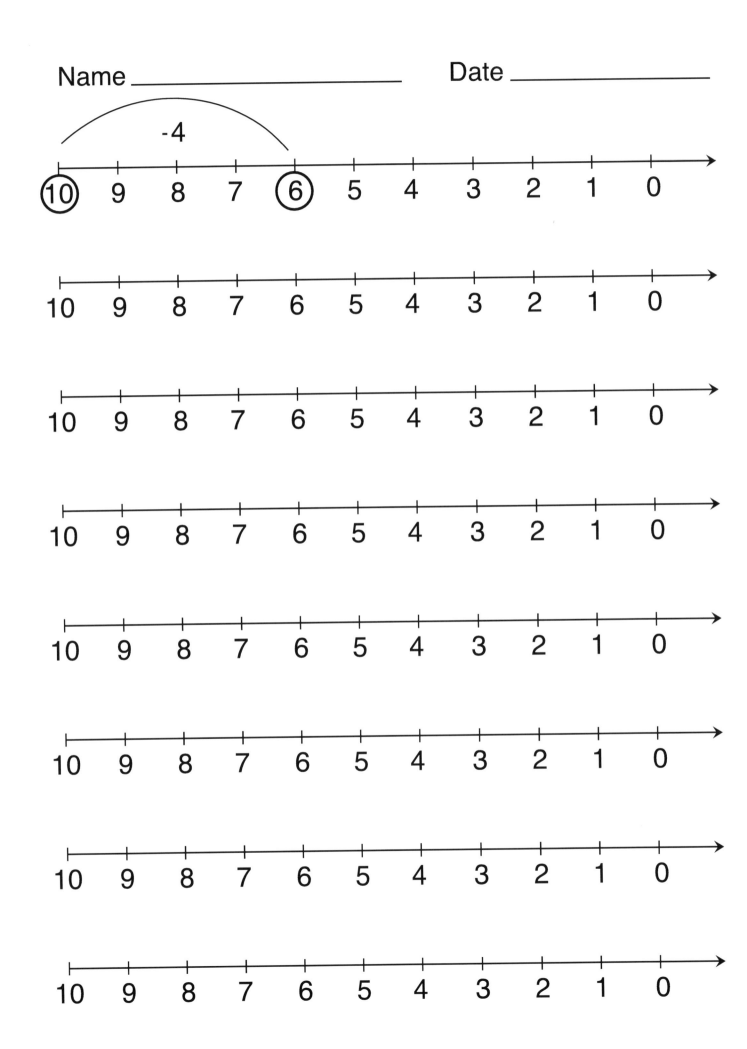

$8 - 1 =$ _____

$15 - 9 =$ _____

$6 - 4 =$ _____

$3 - 3 =$ _____

$14 - 5 =$ _____

$5 - 2 =$ _____

$5 - 5 =$ _____

$15 - 7 =$ _____

$5 - 0 =$ _____

$4 - 3 =$ _____

$10 - 9 =$ _____

$7 - 1 =$ _____

$18 - 9 =$ _____

$10 - 7 =$ _____

$11 - 3 =$ _____

$13 - 4 =$ _____

$8 - 3 =$ _____

$9 - 0 =$ _____

$17 - 9 =$ _____

$3 - 2 =$ _____

Answer Key

$$8 - 1 = \underline{7}$$

$$15 - 9 = \underline{6}$$

$$6 - 4 = \underline{2}$$

$$3 - 3 = \underline{0}$$

$$14 - 5 = \underline{9}$$

$$5 - 2 = \underline{3}$$

$$5 - 5 = \underline{0}$$

$$15 - 7 = \underline{8}$$

$$5 - 0 = \underline{5}$$

$$4 - 3 = \underline{1}$$

$$10 - 9 = \underline{1}$$

$$7 - 1 = \underline{6}$$

$$18 - 9 = \underline{9}$$

$$10 - 7 = \underline{3}$$

$$11 - 3 = \underline{8}$$

$$13 - 4 = \underline{9}$$

$$8 - 3 = \underline{5}$$

$$9 - 0 = \underline{9}$$

$$17 - 9 = \underline{8}$$

$$3 - 2 = \underline{1}$$

199			196	195	194	193	192	191	190
189	188	187		185		183	182	181	180
179	178		176	175	174	173	172		170
169	168	167		165	164	163	162	161	160
159	158	157	156	155		153	152	151	150
149	148	147	146	145	144	143	142	141	140
139	138		136	135		133	132		130
129	128	127	126	125	124		122	121	120
119	118		116	115	114	113	112	111	110
109	108	107	106	105			102	101	100

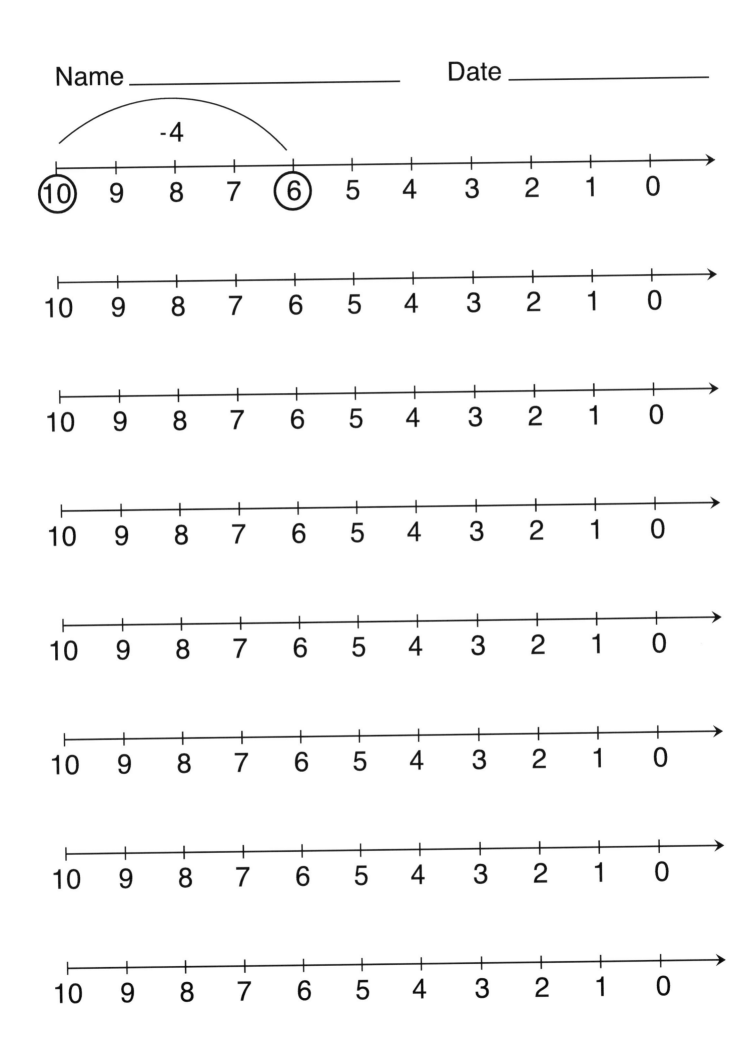

Name _____   Date _____

13 – 5 = _____

12 – 7 = _____

7 – 4 = _____

4 – 0 = _____

3 – 1 = _____

8 – 0 = _____

1 – 1 = _____

5 – 4 = _____

8 – 3 = _____

11 – 3 = _____

10 – 5 = _____

7 – 6 = _____

9 – 2 = _____

15 – 8 = _____

6 – 4 = _____

9 – 4 = _____

5 – 0 = _____

12 – 3 = _____

17 – 9 = _____

12 – 4 = _____

Answer Key

13 – 5 = __8__   12 – 7 = __5__

7 – 4 = __3__   4 – 0 = __4__

3 – 1 = __2__   8 – 0 = __8__

1 – 1 = __0__   5 – 4 = __1__

8 – 3 = __5__   11 – 3 = __8__

10 – 5 = __5__   7 – 6 = __1__

9 – 2 = __7__   15 – 8 = __7__

6 – 4 = __2__   9 – 4 = __5__

5 – 0 = __5__   12 – 3 = __9__

17 – 9 = __8__   12 – 4 = __8__

Name _____ Date _____

199			196	195	194	193	192	191	190
189	188	187	186					181	180
179	178			175	174		172		170
169	168	167		165	164	163	162	161	160
159		157		155	154	153	152	151	150
149	148	147	146	145		143	142	141	140
139	138		136		134	133	132		130
129		127	126	125	124	123	122	121	120
119	118	117		115	114		112	111	110
109	108	107	106	105	104	103	102		

Name _____   Date _____

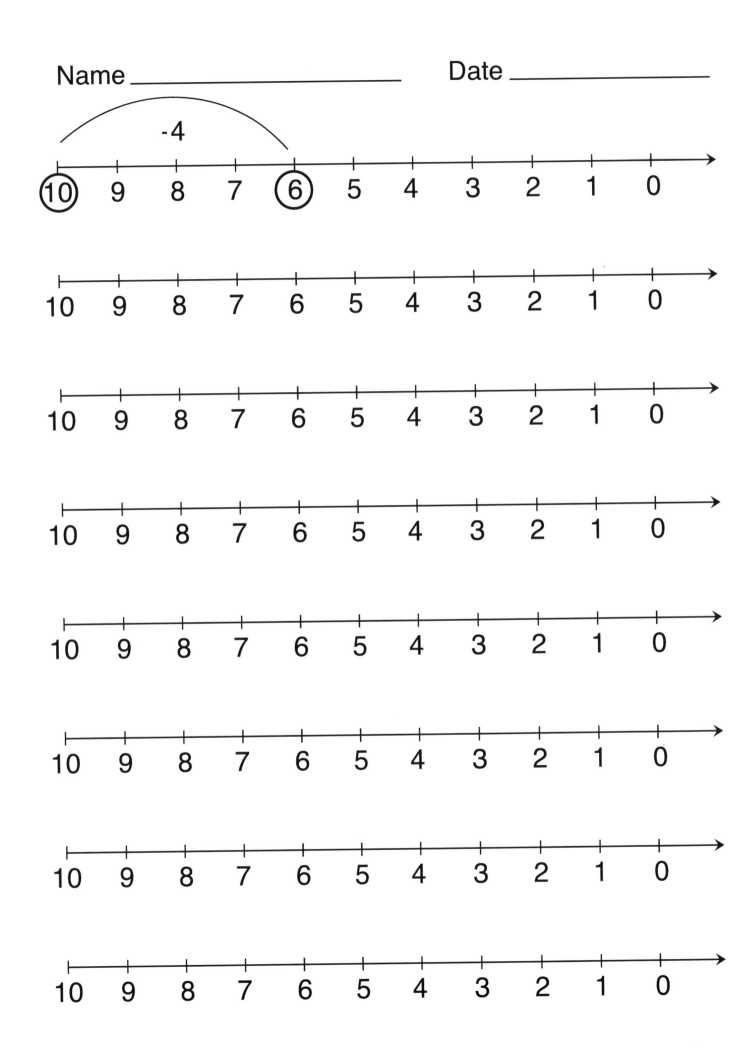

10 – 2 = _____

8 – 2 = _____

10 – 8 = _____

12 – 5 = _____

10 – 6 = _____

7 – 5 = _____

13 – 9 = _____

16 – 7 = _____

14 – 9 = _____

2 – 2 = _____

3 – 1 = _____

5 – 3 = _____

11 – 8 = _____

15 – 6 = _____

1 – 0 = _____

4 – 2 = _____

6 – 0 = _____

9 – 0 = _____

11 – 7 = _____

2 – 1 = _____

Answer Key

$10 - 2 = \underline{8}$

$3 - 1 = \underline{2}$

$8 - 2 = \underline{6}$

$5 - 3 = \underline{2}$

$10 - 8 = \underline{2}$

$11 - 8 = \underline{3}$

$12 - 5 = \underline{7}$

$15 - 6 = \underline{9}$

$10 - 6 = \underline{4}$

$1 - 0 = \underline{1}$

$7 - 5 = \underline{2}$

$4 - 2 = \underline{2}$

$13 - 9 = \underline{4}$

$6 - 0 = \underline{6}$

$16 - 7 = \underline{9}$

$9 - 0 = \underline{9}$

$14 - 9 = \underline{5}$

$11 - 7 = \underline{4}$

$2 - 2 = \underline{0}$

$2 - 1 = \underline{1}$

199				195	194	193	192	191	190
189	188	187					182	181	180
179	178		176	175	174	173	172	171	170
169	168	167			164		162		160
159	158				154		152	151	150
149	148		146	145	144		142		140
139		137	136		134	133	132	131	130
129	128	127		125	124	123	122	121	120
119					114	113	112	111	110
109	108	107	106	105					

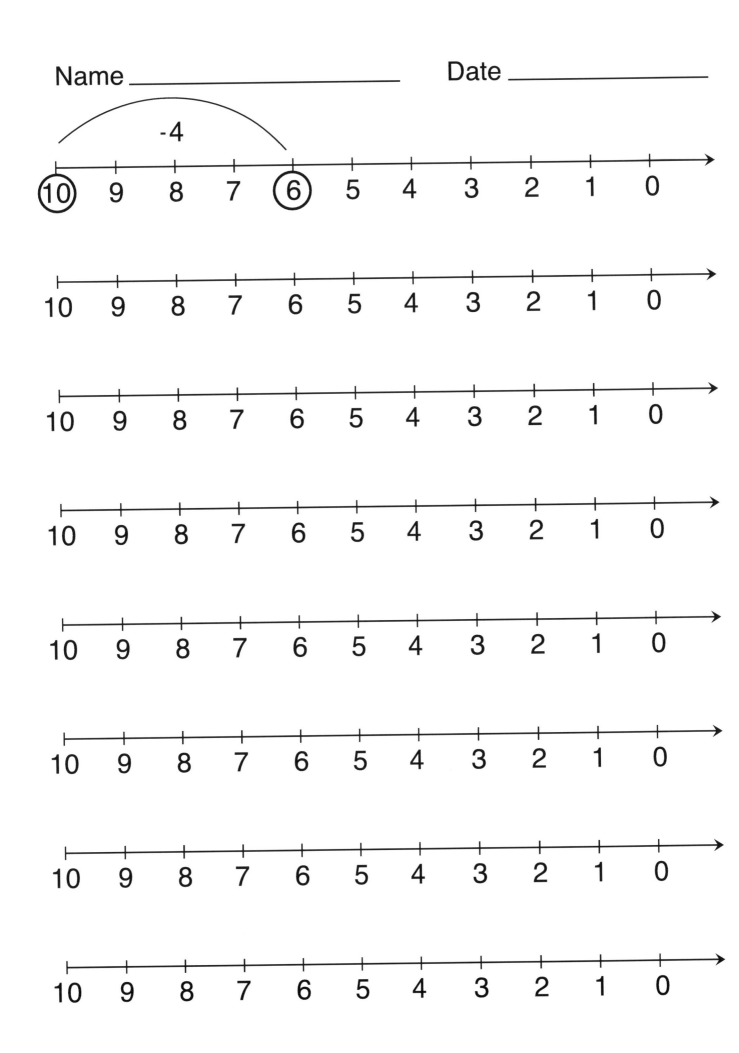

11 – 5 = _____

4 – 1 = _____

10 – 4 = _____

12 – 3 = _____

9 – 1 = _____

3 – 0 = _____

1 – 0 = _____

9 – 9 = _____

9 – 7 = _____

2 – 1 = _____

1 – 1 = _____

9 – 0 = _____

8 – 4 = _____

9 – 2 = _____

13 – 9 = _____

5 – 3 = _____

5 – 4 = _____

6 – 3 = _____

8 – 8 = _____

11 – 6 = _____

Answer Key

$11 - 5 = \underline{6}$

$4 - 1 = \underline{3}$

$10 - 4 = \underline{6}$

$12 - 3 = \underline{9}$

$9 - 1 = \underline{8}$

$3 - 0 = \underline{3}$

$1 - 0 = \underline{1}$

$9 - 9 = \underline{0}$

$9 - 7 = \underline{2}$

$2 - 1 = \underline{1}$

$1 - 1 = \underline{0}$

$9 - 0 = \underline{9}$

$8 - 4 = \underline{4}$

$9 - 2 = \underline{7}$

$13 - 9 = \underline{4}$

$5 - 3 = \underline{2}$

$5 - 4 = \underline{1}$

$6 - 3 = \underline{3}$

$8 - 8 = \underline{0}$

$11 - 6 = \underline{5}$

Name _____ Date _____

199							192	191	
189	188					183	182	181	180
179							172		170
169	168								160
							152	151	150
149		147		145	144	143			
139							132		130
129		127	126						
119	118		116	115				111	110
109		107		105					100

— = _____   — = _____

— = _____   — = _____

— = _____   — = _____

— = _____   — = _____

— = _____   — = _____

— = _____   — = _____

— = _____   — = _____

— = _____   — = _____

— = _____   — = _____

— = _____   — = _____

— = _____   — = _____

— = _____   — = _____

— = _____   — = _____

— = _____   — = _____

— = _____   — = _____

— = _____   — = _____

— = _____   — = _____

— = _____   — = _____

— = _____   — = _____

— = _____   — = _____

— — = _____   — — = _____

— — = _____   — — = _____

— — = _____   — — = _____

— — = _____   — — = _____

— — = _____   — — = _____

— — = _____   — — = _____

— — = _____   — — = _____

— — = _____   — — = _____

— — = _____   — — = _____

— — = _____   — — = _____

Name _____ Date _____

— = _____   — = _____

— = _____   — = _____

— = _____   — = _____

— = _____   — = _____

— = _____   — = _____

— = _____   — = _____

— = _____   — = _____

— = _____   — = _____

— = _____   — = _____

— = _____   — = _____

— = _____   — = _____

— = _____   — = _____

— = _____   — = _____

— = _____   — = _____

— = _____   — = _____

— = _____   — = _____

— = _____   — = _____

— = _____   — = _____

— = _____   — = _____

— = _____   — = _____

— = _____   — = _____

— = _____   — = _____

— = _____   — = _____

— = _____   — = _____

— = _____   — = _____

— = _____   — = _____

— = _____   — = _____

— = _____   — = _____

— = _____   — = _____

— = _____   — = _____

— = _____   — = _____

— = _____   — = _____

— = _____   — = _____

— = _____   — = _____

— = _____   — = _____

— = _____   — = _____

— = _____   — = _____

— = _____   — = _____

— = _____   — = _____

— = _____   — = _____

SPI MATH WORKBOOKS

1st GRADE

Builds and boosts key skills

Includes:

+ Math Drills
+ Number Counting
+ Addition Lines

Name_____ Date_____

BASIC MATH DRILLS

1+3=4   1+4=5
8+1=9   7+1=8
_=5   2+1=3
2+4=7   3+3=6

If you enjoyed this book. Please check out Basic Math Drills (Addition)

46582513R00029

Made in the USA
San Bernardino, CA
07 August 2019